A Bracken Fern
Selected Poems 2020-2025

First published in 2025
by Experiments in Fiction
All rights reserved

© Ingrid Wilson, 2025

Ingrid Wilson is hereby identified as author of this work
ISBN-13: 978-1-7394044-8-2

A BRACKEN FERN
Selected Poems 2020-2025

by the same author

40 POEMS AT 40
EIF, 2022

ARCHERY IN THE UK
with Nick Reeves
EIF, 2023

TO CATCH A POEM
EIF, 2023

Ingrid Wilson

A BRACKEN FERN

Selected Poems 2020-2025

Experiments In Fiction

Dedicated to the memory of my Mother,
Elizabeth Mary Clare Stakle (née Wilson).

"The eagle never lost so much time
as when he submitted to learn of the crow."
—William Blake, *Proverbs of Hell*, c.1790

"You fail only when you let death creep in and take over a
part of your life that should be alive."
—Bob Dylan, 1977

Contents

No Homelike Place	15
Brown into Green	17
Poem on your Birthday	18
My Father's Garden	19
In Flight	20
Sorry, Mate…	22
Slow Sleepwalk into Armageddon	24
Earth-Mother	26
Siren Song	27
Warm Saharan Winds	28
Points North	30
Blake: An Ode	32
Jellyfish Jam	34
The Earth Does Not Look Sick	36
Do Not Look for Me There	37
When Spring Flowers…	38
Serpentine	39
Persephone	40
Star of Wonder	41
You and Me, Sea	43
Bear Witness	45
A Thimble of Poetry	47
Dawn Resonance	49
Seedhead Hope Song	50
When the Named Storms Come	51
If You Kill the Bird	53

Watershed	54
Winter's Margin	55
Windswept	56
Heiress	57
Park Broom	58
Tao of the Wind	59
Epiphany, 2024	60
Burns Night, 2024	61
Ranging	62
Kindred	63
Henge Complex	65
Oddendale	66
On Burnswark Hill	67
Northern Wilds	68
Wind-painted	70
All the Way to Midsummer	71
A Day of Frets and Seagulls	73
Arboreal	74
Where I Belong	75
One in a Vermilion	76
Walking the Wall	77
Without	78
Turner Skies	79
The Mirror	80
Trespass	82
Autumn on the Northeast Coast of England	83
Pantoum for a Northern Autumn	85
I Stand with the Trees	86

Beachcombing	87
Shunyata	89
Along the Winding Trail	90
Mulholland Drive is Burning	91
The Engraver's Art	92
Emily	93
Last Ride before Easter	95
Petrarchan Sonnet	97
Of Molehills…	98
Wholly Holy Island	99
Streets of Dreaming	100
A Bracken Fern	102
Child of the Wild High Places	104
Through Rising Tides	105
Long Live "No-neck"	107
If I Could Paint the Colours of your Eyes	108
Unlearned	109
Banded	110
Devoke	111
The Quickening	112
Softly, over Skiddaw	113
Publication Credits	115

No Homelike Place

There is no homelike place,
only an empty space
where once the toys were piled:
A legend, etched in pencil on a wall,
growth of a child
meticulously charted, inch by inch
and line by loving line
too easily erased.

There is no homelike place:
all whitewashed now
the memories.
Perhaps a paltry palimpsest survives
beneath the pale magnolia emulsion
records of past lives
remain for years
beneath the stains of nicotine and tears.

There is no homelike place, only
hotel rooms on the road:
Nameless places
homeless, faceless
searching for a place to call one's own,
a harbour, or a home
or somewhere warm at least, at best
a homelike place.

There is no homelike place
for children of addiction and abuse
whose carers breached the sanctity of dreams
and stole the sanctuary
of playgrounds, of the nursery and school;
who, for their selfish, careless use
stole childhood, leaving them
no homelike place.

Praying we can find
a homelike place
we build our houses,
sink squat castles in the sand, erect
grand palaces and mansions
and we say we are secure,
but we can never build without
the homelike place
which we must seek, and find and build
within ourselves, which nowhere else endures.

2020

Brown into Green

Brown fleck
in a green eye:
Something rare, I got the green,
the thickness of your hair,
my children got the
hazel-brown
so maybe
in that fleck
there was encoded, double-helix style
a spark of life
which carried on from you
to me
to them
and now I see
with mother's eyes
the way you used to see.
And yes, I'm tired.
And yes, I struggle sometimes, still
at the heart of it all
eyes see
[and all
I see
is] love.

2020

Poem on your Birthday

I remember
the coolness of your skin, and your warm heart
the thickness of your hair, and your thin body
seemed like the wind could blow right through you
which it did
as it blows through me now, though
it won't blow me over.

I remember
you waiting for me in the school yard,
at my favourite time of day,
and the days you didn't come:
The worst,
and the one day you would never come again,
a nightmare.

Still, in time there are wild flowers again
and sunny days.
There is new life, new love
and still the old, which never left:
It's blowing in the wind
which blows through you
and blows through all things, but cannot destroy
our love.

2020

My Father's Garden

My father's garden is overgrown,
a jungle of wild flowers from
my mother's time.
She loved the wilderness, transplanted it:
It bloomed because of her
green-fingered magic.
I feel it still:
My favourites are the peonies which bloom
each June, ephemeral
brightest of all.

2020

In Flight

Fly high, little bird,
swallow on the wing,
swift as you circle,
soft as you sing.

Fly free, little bird,
head into the wind,
deftly descending,
fodder to find.

Glide high, soaring bird,
drift on the air,
catching the thermals,
hovering there.

Hunt well, little bird,
soaring bird, too,
one feeds on earthworms
the other, on you:

No flight is for free
on this tooth-and-claw earth
for all have to feed
even in times of dearth.

Feed well, little bird
soaring bird, too,
bringing scraps to your nest
this life to continue:

Even so, fly,
if I could, I'd be free
as you seem, without care,
not grow hungry and die.

2020

Sorry, Mate...

As I sank into the depths of alcoholism
depression and despair
not a soul around me seemed to care
except the man who stood next to me on the tube
whose eyes seemed to declare, 'How dare
you stand so close to me?'
Perhaps I didn't smell too good:

Sorry, Mate, did I spoil your commute?

The Councilmen evicted me
because I couldn't pay the rent:
Nothing else for it then but to be
drunk on a park bench at 8am.
A cyclist whizzed past me,
in a hurry, still
he somehow found the time to spit
in my general direction:

Sorry, Mate, did I spoil your commute?

Traffic's circulating on the M25 quite nicely
and it gives me a grim satisfaction
as I climb the stairs and wait:
I have pick my exit time just right.
I used to drive this route myself,

I had a company car like you
and like you I would get pissed off,
when some tosser would climb the bridge and throw
himself off.
So I bequeath to you my final thought:

Sorry, Mate, did I spoil your commute?

2020

Slow Sleepwalk into Armageddon

It was a sweet walk, where we once held hands
and danced,
a waltz around the wilting wheatfields
imagining that we still had a chance:
Slow sleepwalk into Armageddon
like dying flames of a once-wild romance.

Slow sleepwalk into Armageddon like
a fevered dream
delirious and staggering
and tossed like whirling twigs within a stream
of consciousness,
unconscious of the brink to which we'd come

till we went over. Down and down we fell!
Some had the nerve to cry 'What have we done
to deserve this?'
While others knew the answer all too well:
Slowly, we'd sleep-walked into Armageddon,
transforming all the bounty of the Earth
into a living Hell.

2020

Jerusalem's Lament

After Blake's 'Jerusalem'

Jerusalem—where are you now?
Jerusalem—where did you go?
Sunk in those dark, satanic mills?
Adrift amid the springtime snow?

Where is that green and pleasant land
where once we raised our hymn of praise?
Where is the sunkissed golden strand
we visited on brighter days?

And if those feet in ancient times
once walked here, they were welcome not
to linger: Foreign footsteps here
are seldom praised, but driven out.

Even the Holy Lamb of God
was slaughtered where the trees once stood
all in the name of progress, to the greater good
of markets, we draw further blood.

2020

Earth-Mother

Snake-charmer
Goddess—voluptuous
viper—venomous
whisperer—livewire lover.

Original author
immaculate sinner
sorceress—temptress
seductress and mentor.

Thunderbolt-wielder,
bounteous-Mother
Earth-spitting venom now breaking asunder:

You shouldn't have crossed her!
You shouldn't have crossed her!
Now cross your own heart
and admit that it's over:

Cross your heart
hope to die
painlessly.

2020

Siren Song

Sing on, sweet Muse, of my lost love;
so far away he waits for me;
sing on sweet Muse of my lost love
and I'll sing him to me.

A thousand miles away he waits
beyond the sea, beyond the pale
and I would sing him home to me:
Let words not fail.

I wait upon this barren rock;
the spray hits hard, salt stings my tears
through many a storm and many a wreck
through thoughtless, restless years.

How thoughtless you, not to return
while here I wait upon my rock;
how heartless you, not to return:
Now, let me sing you back.

I see your ship upon the waves,
your ship draws near as I draw breath;
I sing my song to bring you close:
My song shall be your death.

2020

Warm Saharan Winds

Warm Saharan winds
blow from the south in summer
ceaselessly
releasing
unrelenting heat.

Warm Saharan winds
blew spices of Morocco
and dances
free and wild
into Iberia.

Warm Saharan winds
like hot breath
on the scorched earth
speak of a sandstorm
in a far-off land.

Warm Saharan winds
in summer blow through
all our lives
and all our doubts
and fears.

Warm Saharan winds
which leave us sleepless through

the breathless night
and on into the dawn, still
too soon gone.

2020

Points North

Wheels in motion, and the wind
whips around behind my ears,
at the nape of my neck
in a subtle caress
and I know I'm being propelled
along a river of life
whose course and motion
I do not pretend to understand:
Sometimes I like it when the waters
speed me down towards a sea
sunless and sighing

until the cloud breaks
and I see
the sky is crying.
And at sundown
out come all the thousand stars,
and I can name the constellations
in this hemisphere
at any time of year:
There is always The Plough
above, or 'The Big Dipper'
and at its tip, Polaris
The Pole Star
points North.

And so I have my fixed
celestial compass,
though I do not
always understand the path
or the trajectory,
I know well my own
portion of the sky:
The earth below, above only the heavens and
Points North.

2020

Blake: An Ode

After Blake's 'The Tyger'

In what furnace was thy brain
forged? What adamantine blade
cut those mind forg'd manacles
and freed you?

Freed, into the vales of Har
th' eternal porter lifts the bar
the Garden of Love opens, read
'Though shalt' over the door:

Thou shalt write in darkness
only to shine, with the engraver's art.
Thou shalt enlighten every one of us
who seeks to know thine heart.

And when that heart has ceased to beat
what dread poem, to what dread beat
shall follow, in your fearful wake
the world to rouse, its core to shake?

Blake! We are sleepwalking!
Blake! Caught within mills with complicated wheels!
Blake! my only hope:
If we persist long enough in such folly
we may yet become wise

as you envisioned in your prophecy.[1]

2021

---

[1] This poem also includes references to 'London,' *The Book of Thel,* 'The Garden of Love,' and *The Marriage of Heaven and Hell.*

Jellyfish Jam

Jellyfish jam
sugar-coated with spam
'But I'm already dead'
the jellyfish said:

'I'm your mushroom-cloud
polyurethane shroud
and I'm blooming without
while within there's a drought

and it isn't your fault;
it was never your fault:
You were such a success
populating this mess!

But I'm taking my leave,
there'll be time yet to grieve
for my kind when we're gone
and the ocean's forlorn.

But your doubts and your fears,
can you drown them with tears?
Like you've drowned your own kind,
I'd say, time out of mind.

Jellyfish jam
still, I am what I am
as I just before said,
I am already dead.'

2021

The Earth Does Not Look Sick

The Earth does not look sick
on days like these
it looks perfectly healthy:
Replete with rich resources,
indefatigable bounty;
yet I fear it is not so.

When the land burns,
we look out to sea
and say, 'it isn't so.'
When the sea starves and swells,
we look to higher ground,
oblivious to warnings

until we are brought face to face
one fateful morning:
Stranded on a patch of beach,
behind the burning land, beyond
the sea, salvation
out of reach.

2021

Do Not Look for Me There

I am not in the ground,
do not look for me there:
I am the gentle wind that caresses your hair
in summer.

I am the spring tide rising before crashing to the shore;
I am the spring light that kisses your face
and what's more
I'm everywhere.

2021

When Spring Flowers...

I shall not pass this way again
but if you should, in sun or rain
or when spring flowers bedeck the grass,
remember me, where your feet pass
and shed a tear, in happiness
for all once dear, though passed in us
is limitless.

2021

Serpentine

Serpentine, I'd like to make you mine:
You shouldn't wonder
would I pull you under?
Just take it slow,
my waters flow like wine.

You picnickers and panickers
nit-picking at your children by the river:
I could make you forget all your cares—
I'm timeless, baby,
won'tcha come on over?

See the spirits sunbathing on the shore?
They swam into my swirl
like twigs a-twirling.
And see my lady with the serpent's tail?
She's oh-so fine, her velvet hair unfurling.

And me? I've been here since the dawn of time
and to the end I'll linger,
face still like stone,
statuesque, serpentine:
River spirit, life-giving dead-ringer.

2021

Persephone

Sunk deep into the dark half of the year
Persephone lies weeping underground,
and no one watches where she sheds a tear
for distant spring, when she shall rise, unbound.

Hades' love transformed into loathing,
though she's loathed him through centuries long gone,
and all the earth is dressed in winter clothing
in barren fields, where once spring lambs were born.

'Why weep for winter? Do not weep for me!'
She cries into the miles of ground above.
Fathoms below, she hears the sighing sea,
and dries her tears with dreams of summer love.

The hibernation of all joy awaits
spring resurrected: She shall not be late.

2021

Star of Wonder

Star of Wonder:
Light in the children's eyes,
around the tree
abound our hopes and memories.

I dream of childhood
without dread or fear,
long-gone December days
haunting my always.

Away in a Manger
we hear that once a baby slept
embraced in love
into our lives He crept.

We were not ready
for His message, then
no more than now:
Oh come, Emanuel
and save us, anyhow.

The earth is burning,
all the windtorn trees are down,
Earth spirits, turning
look on our wanton work of death, and mourn.

So, come, Lord Jesus
and show us how to face our fate, ordained
even as we're washed out on the tide
to love without restraint.

2021

You and Me, Sea

Ain't it just like you and me, Sea
when we dance together,
I barefoot on the sand, you
lapping at my toes?

Ain't it just like we're two parts of
the same whole:
I was born of you, and you
bring me to life once more?

Ain't it just like you and me, Sea?
And we've always been together
dancing a saline tango in the sun.

Ain't it just like you and me, Sea?
When I hit stormy weather
on your shore I'll wind up, by the wild winds
flung.

Say, it's just like you and me, Sea,
I can hear you calling:
Your echo fills my silent afternoon.

And that was all I wanted to say, Sea:
When I'm far away from you
I feel your surge in me, which swells into
a tide to take me home.

2021

Bear Witness

The broken bodies of trees catch in the weir
carried by currents swirling blackly,
like the current that carried your broken body here:
Bear witness to the falling of the trees.

34 years of life transformed overnight
to 32 (and counting) years of grief.
Can nature or nurture offer some relief?
If so, then let still-standing trees bear witness.

Each fallen tree's more than a hundred years to grieve
it's passing, ring by ancient ring
we cannot look the other way, they block our path, we must
bear witness to the falling of the trees.

These griefs and losses that we carry with us:
A mother gone, a childhood up in flames,
burn back into a something else, a stillness
this, let still standing trees bear witness

is our last clue, last hope: Humanity
weft into nature's healing tapestry,
a song of love, a line of poetry
bears witness to the falling of the trees.

And sometimes I believe there is a way
between the corpses of the fallen trees:
The light of unimagined hope has found us, we
let the still-standing trees bear witness.

2022

A Thimble of Poetry

"He went to sea in a thimble of poetry."—Jim Harrison,
Poet Warning

He cast off early
just as dawn was breaking,
saw the blues there, saw the greens,
dreamed the clouds were Kingdoms ruled
by distant Kings and Queens.

He'd often wondered
what it took to get there:
This airy realm, this realm of mist and ice,
to feel the cloudburst on his skin
like breath of paradise.

He cast his net wide,
took in sea-brack, blown-in
flotsam, things that people leave
out on the beach to travel with
the tide's incessant weave.

He wove their stories
like a winter cloak, hardwearing
weathered with fabled centuries,
from pieces of their lives he made
enduring histories.

He wrote mine down too:
Wrote it down and sung it
wistful, dreaming on the breeze
that somehow it might reach my heart
beyond those swelling seas.

2022

Dawn Resonance

Beneath my window, soft birdsong
plays in my garden, all along
the treeline: Sweet, melodic, low
'For I have lovéd you so long,'
the lyric chimes with sounds below:
Soft birdsong beneath my window.

As I awake from this sweet dream
warmed from within, though no sunbeam
appears, its dawning breath to take
without a dazzle or a gleam
I drink you in, my thirst to slake
from this sweet dream, as I awake.

I am so fortunate to find
space to pen love songs in my mind
while outside day is growing late:
The school bell beckons on the wind
and duty calls me to the gate
to find I am so fortunate.

2022

Seedhead Hope Song

Derwentwater's oaken shore
gives onto waters, crystal pure
or so they were, now marred with foam:
A plague upon my mountain home!

Bracken-clad hillsides' colours change
with seasons as they rearrange
and sphagnum moss and cotton-grass
wet walker's bootsteps where they pass

as yew and sedge and ash trees bend
in winds which blow, the boughs to rend,
while birdsong of the lark and thrush
ascends with a melodious rush

into the upper atmosphere:
Some clearer, brighter, sweeter air.
Our hopes, though fragile, rising high
as dandelion-seeds dance the sky.

2022

When the Named Storms Come

When the named storms come
and the power lines are down
and our channels of communication have been cut
how will you contact me?

I will be reaching out to you, and you
will mirror me, who reaches out
even now, even as I write this
in the dark.

When the named storms come
again, you'll send a letter:
I am sure you will
and hope the postal service doesn't falter

and I will write a poem
like lovers did in bygone times
and seal it in a lipsticked envelope
addressed in my inked hand.

And if the post can't make it through
then I will drive to you
and if I can't get petrol
I will ride my bike

from coast to coloured coast
and you will greet me on the bridge
at mouth of Tyne, our lips will meet
after the storm is done:

I will still love you when the named storms come.

2022

If You Kill the Bird

"You're just an empty cage, girl, if you kill the bird."—
Tori Amos, Crucify

If you kill the bird
you'll rise up every morning
drone-like, yawning
heart un-singing.

If you kill the bird
you'll spend your whole life mourning
yearning, wishing:
Unfulfilling.

If you kill the bird
you're dead girl, walking
empty streets through hard
rain falling:

You're just an empty cage girl
void of poetry, unheard,
you're just an empty cage girl
if you kill
you kill the bird.

2022

Watershed

I know the name
of every mountain in these lands
lay my hands on granite rock
and sphagnum moss,
spongy lungs of this rich earth,
terrain I cross

to walk the wind along the watershed
of Derwent and Eden,
lean into skies, buffeted like a tree
still standing, through a curtain of ice rain
almost to heaven's edge
and back again.

I hug the leeward of Bannerdale Crags
pretend to wend my way back home
yet not so,
for other paths I know
and one half of my wanderer's heart
remains to roam.

2022

Winter's Margin

Shades of the prison house
exist within the shadows,
lurk at the peripheries
of winter's margin.

Our birth is but a sleep
and a forgetting[1]—what?
The light, from which we came
still burns within.

Cold bites, the penniless poets
strike a match,
burn incense, cup wax candles in star-jars,
draw closer in.

Your hands recall the sculptor's art
of Michelangelo
and I know all past glories of this earth
await some parallel, hidden rebirth

beyond the edge of time
the porter lifts the northern bar[2]
and spring pours in remembered light
at winter's margin.   *2022*

---

1   Wordsworth, 'Intimations of Immortality...'
2   Blake, *Book of Thel*

Windswept

Wind swept the doorstep
brushed the autumn leaves away,
well-kept, not unkempt
like rumours of a yesterday

unlocked, the hall clock
rounds up all the old flock
standing silent by the wall
with never a "tick-tock"

in time, the wind chimes
aspirate these old rhymes
breathed into life by firelight
falling on our parlour games

rain-drenched, the park bench,
where once lovers, thirst-quenched
carved a legend of love
on wood worn and wind-blanched

bone-still, through nights, chill
and dark, by the old sill
she sits nigh, with glass eye
now windswept, her bones, still.

2023

Heiress

I am an Heiress,
I am a Queen,
below, beneath, without, within
the wind that shakes the windowpane:
Between, between, between!

I, an Enchantress
calling your name
on a distant hillside at high noon
beneath the waxing, waning moon:
In tune, in tune, in tune.

I am the Huntress
chasing you down
through trackless forest
overgrown
you run, but still I find you here:
Alone, alone, alone!

I know your secret,
I know you best,
with timeless insight I am blessed,
party to all the pain you caused:
Confess, confess, confess!

2023

Park Broom

The journey seems to take almost forever,
despite the fast-flowing currents of the water
from Wetheral, to Park Broom down the river

where, in your wake, wandering, walks a daughter
trying to piece the afterlife together
from Wetheral, to Park Broom down the river.

Thirty-three years is long enough to wonder
about the current which carried you under
Broomy Hill to Park Broom down the river:

Follow the trail, then stop a while and ponder
the hills beyond, which stood beneath the thunder
the day they found you, lying in the water.

And I would plunge my hands, right then and there
into the bright, flowing darkness of the river
to piece your broken body back together.

2023

Tao of the Wind

"When you speak it is silent, when you are silent, it speaks" – Lao Tse, Tao Te Ching

Tao of the wind
Tao of the rain
Tao of the moon and stars

Tao of the hungry
Tao of the angry
Tao of Venus and Mars

Tao of the war-torn
Tao of the peaceful
Tao of the days and years

Tao of the wasteful
Tao of the careful
Tao of the smiles and tears

Tao of these words
Tao of their absence
Tao of my joys and fears.

2023

Epiphany, 2024

All is calm, all is bright
all is mirror, mist and light:
All is magic, all perception
polished, in the lake's reflection.

All is wonder, all is well
all is ancient symbol, spell
the mountain circle, golden ring
spins so, the land begins to sing.

Ancient music, modern muse
lie of the land, the lay you choose
to weave your wisdom of the hills
and sing of rivers, streams and rills:

A clockwork candle, telling time
though waxed in shadow, light, sublime
that all upon Epiphany
with opened eyes at last, might see.

2024

Burns Night, 2024

Ghost of a sunset in the western sky,
ranks of Roman soldiers to my left,
a tarmac-ribbon, stretching, asphalt grey
towards my home, with nature's warp and weft

followed, as the full moon peeps through cloudbreaks
to strands of Beethoven and static cling:
Between these strains of universal music
stranger voices sing.

I'm riding, high above the landscape
dear to me, beloved Borderland,
safe from the dazzle of incessant headlights
ancient ways I wend

and, in the roar of the winds, I hear
the song of centuries: Of balladeers'
wee, *tim'rous* and *cowran*[3] voices
growing strong, resounding loud and clear.

2024

---

3   Robbie Burns, 'To A Mouse'

Ranging

Ranging, over these northern hills,
soaring high above their streams and rills:
Your touch transports me to a land beyond
this cold, dark earth, becoming hallowed ground

swept back, so to reveal the starry sky,
above the ley-lined land, for you and me.
Dancing, reeling the circle round,
weaving between the flowers, where they're found:

Footsteps so soft you would not know we'd been
here since the days of song on earth began,
and slowly we dance beyond the earth below
returning home, to light the sky tomorrow.

2024

Kindred

On Moor Divock, rising
the Lake District round,
millennia passing
above the hard ground

beneath: Water, dancing
ice carved this land
scrying, surfacing
where these stones stand.

The Pennines, to their east
mark a watershed
between ancient landscapes
whose secrets are hid

for those who would find them:
Pilgrims to the stones
where once, circled mounds
softly covered the bones

of the people who built them
and dreamed beneath skies
which have altered but little
through these centuries:

And I think of the kindred
who left us their mark
to be gleaned in the daytime,
alight in the dark.

2024

Henge Complex

A pebbled bank reveals a hidden hollow
within the ring, one standing stone remains.
Sheep nibble grass, where sometime pilgrims follow
ancient clues, and wonder at the finds:

Fingerprint traces, earthworks overgrown
with grass, and time, amnesia and mist;
manicured, resembling a lawn,
a village green, King Arthur's holy quest

perhaps began here, in the mythic mind
but elders, in more distant times than this
had watched the stars, in ever-changing motion
and left behind these earthworks to bear witness.

2024

Oddendale

Ode
& dale,
and song and vale
where sounds rebound
throughout these chambered
mounds
of earth
which, covered since their birth
are now revealed
in lines which led me
here
I lie
beneath the open sky:
A Wanderer
A Warrior
A Pilgrim Child
am I.

2024

On Burnswark Hill

Every layer they strip/Seems camped on before — Seamus Heaney, 'Bogland'

A place I'd wondered at, but never visited:
Threshold of the silty Solway plain,
a table-mountain, hill-fort, watershed
of coastal grasslands, washed with gentle rain.

Viewing-platform, vistas roll endlessly
over lush pastures to the fells beyond
which form a border on the southwest sky
leaving me silent, spirited, spellbound:

To finally stand here, and to know the name
after so many years of wondering,
another territory I may claim
within the landscape of my homecoming.

*Each compass point meets here where time stands still
encompassing past lives, my life: This hill.*

2024

Northern Wilds

Tinnis Hill
Cristianbury Crags
Tower Brae:
Broad sweep of the North,
wild homelands to me.

For miles and miles
only rolling hills
and few
have passed this way:

And those who passed were pilgrims
from unremembered time
to honour the dead
they'd laid beneath
this silent mountainside.

And those who roamed were Romans
whose forts and lookout posts
staked out their claim to these wild lands
from coast to shining coast.

And those who carried Cuddy
over this vast wilderness
from East to West
then South

to lay
his saint's body to rest.

And those who love the silence,
the singing of the wind,
the cool cry of the cuckoo,
these are my humankind.

2024

Wind-painted

Wind-painted
hand-tinted,
along the Firth, the evening light is splintered

half-hidden
unbidden
beneath the rocks, the ancestors, bed-ridden

speak secrets
sink trinkets
deep into earth, whose rich peat warms, and blankets:

Sleep, sister
all winter
till sunflowers rise to greet the skies of summer.

2024

All the Way to Midsummer

All the way to Midsummer
the birds sing me awake, while the trees dance
and flowering buds burst open, wet with dew
the cuckoo sings,
ku-koo! ku-koo!
Call and response
which brings me home
to you.

All the way to midday, through
the middens like a maiden in the sands
I pick through tidepools searching waters clear
to find a gift
perfect, spendthrift
a pearl-oyster
to show my love
so dear.

All the way to midnight, I
watch full moons rise if only in your eyes.
It's more than moonlight, babe, it's starlight, too
and earth expands
in your cupped hands
our wedding bands
in secret pledge
I do.

All the way to nowhere in
particular, yet everywhere I find
engraved, ingrained, inkstained traces of you:
I follow streams
cross rail-track beams
and mountain seams
to tell my love
so true.

2024

A Day of Frets and Seagulls

It was a day of frets and seagulls,
of seared and sunburnt clouds,
of starling picnics,
hovering and hungry crowds.

Clouds burned back into summer
hillsides rolling, glorious and green,
a landscape painted
by a hand bold, yet unseen.

It was a day of love and laughter:
Coffee cups and chocolate crumbs,
sticky and melting,
licked from hungry thumbs.

It was a hand held fast and firmly,
candyfloss skies, and seaside promenades:
A day of endless summer
avenues and bright arcades.

2024

Arboreal

Huge phosphorescences flashed across the sky
for all the world to see:

The birds sang to the sunset in the east
The birds sang to the sunset in the west

The bluebells spilled their way all down the hills
in rivulets and rills:

The birds sang to the morning in the trees
The birds sang to the humming of the bees

While oak and ash spread out their canopy
above and over me:

The birds sang, "this is all the life there is"
the birds sang, "who needs heaven, more than this?"

2024

Where I Belong

The millrace, the mud and the midsummer sun,
which sets into red sandstone, moonlight and song,
that chatters and chirrups and moans all night long
over the hillside to where I belong.

The sea and the sand, and the swell of the tide
which surges and swirls as it casts its net wide,
retreating, retracting just as I'm reborn
I'll follow the coastline to where I belong:

In clover, all over the meadow at dawn
I rest in the grass and the dew of the lawn
and always, in all ways, I know I am home
lying here, close to earth, which is where I belong.

2024

One in a Vermilion

What's the colour of the lake at sunset?
Is it crimson?
Scarlet?
One-in-a-vermilion?
Like a soap I used to covet,
as I held it to the sunlight like a lens?

It's the colour of the mountains in December,
nearing evening
rosy-cheeked: An alabaster maid.

Lure of the day's last light,
lurid, ultraviolet,
passionate, inviolate:
The colour of a bedframe set on fire.

Then, we cross the ragged wire
fence, as the reed sea parts
over sodden boots, and

on the asphalt at the edge of twilight
we both hold the *one-in-a-vermilion*
intangible,
a mirror for our hearts.

2024

Walking the Wall

Walking the Wall, which straddles centuries
from west to east, to you, always to you.
Sheltering from fierce winds, as the storm's incendiary
lightning sparks the poles between us two.

It's windy on the Wall tonight, it's raining,
It's cold along the Wall, under moonshine
but meet me on the Wall, when all is shining:
I'll kiss away your blues, for you are mine.

Ghost-soldiers man the turrets and milecastles,
ghost-wives pen letters, sheltered in the fort
Walking the Wall, I still face my own battles:
Would persevere through flood, or fire, or drought.

Yet without you, such journeying's in vain:
I walk the Wall to meet you in the rain.

2024

Without

From the carriage window
heading into the city
detachedly, unhurriedly I see

*the people without
and the people who have
the people who take
and the people who leave:*

Youth on the grass
fingers each passing train
protesting nothing, all in vain

*like the people who shout
and the people who curse
those who quietly wait
their life's fortune's reverse*

as the terraces give onto
box-house estates,
rows and rows of pearly gates

*keep the people within
and all beauty without
tarmacked over in vain
through the cracks, bursting out.*   *2024*

Turner Skies

Turner skies,
sandcastle days,
and shells, strung out like rosaries
adorn our lives,
stretch out for miles,
awake to living ecstasies.

At dawn, we rise
sing hymns of praise
upon the shore, down on our knees,
and, thus inspired
continue, fired
to ever greater reveries.

We build in sand,
we build in air,
in realms unreachable and fair
to say we dream
in pale sunbeams
which haunt the skies, and hover there.

2024

The Mirror

The clouds peel back, revealing the antediluvian roll
of Arthur's Pike
Loadpot Hill
Swarthbeck Gill:

The lake is a mirror
on the sky,
the road is a river,
where cars sail by

rising, to pass by Kirkstone, down to Windermere
where all is calm
all is bright
all is clear.

The lake is a mirror
for the sun
whose smile spreads wide
when evening comes

calling, anvil-like, into the night
over Rydal
Grasmere
sheer delight:

The lake is a mirror
it does not lie
echoing dreams
of earth and sky.

Falling for you over fish and chips, wet lips
sip cola
bowled over
time slips:

Just look in the mirror,
it does not lie,
the lake is a mirror
of yours and my
loving.

2024

Trespass

Trespass on an autumn day:
Forsake the path, and follow me
beyond the hedgerow boundary
and broad beech tree.

Trespass through the new-tilled fields
the cracked, churned earth in spots reveals
past lives, stories of shard and shield
here, unconcealed.

Trespass through hedge, and through barbed wire
emerging by the needle-spire
to circle round its pedestal
and stoke the fire.

2024

Autumn on the Northeast Coast of England

Green sewer-gas lamps
and days of endless damp
as Autumn turns to leaf-mould on the ground.
Clouds rise like vapours
while fish and chip papers
are tossed to the lost and the found.

Ghosts crowd the hall,
arrive for the ball,
they've waited silently all summer long.
The dance begins slowly,
it gathers pace boldly:
A spectral quartet plays along.

The sluice-tide is high
like the waves in the Bay
which crash into the cliffs with their full force:
The harvest is done
and the leaves are all gone
as the Fall of the year runs its course.

It's late afternoon
as my love hums a tune:
We seek shelter at home from the rain.
There is laughter and light
and the candle, so bright

breathes life to my words once again.

2024

Pantoum for a Northern Autumn

Clouds cover sleeping suburban rooftops
ranked in rows below a northern sky:
The wind sighs once, a solitary leaf drops
glints of gold beneath the canopy.

Ranked in rows below a northern sky,
rails stretch out almost to vanishing
glints of gold beneath the canopy,
tidings of magpies, hunt-and-gathering.

Rails stretch out almost to vanishing
points of light pinprick the velvet sky.
Tidings of magpies, hunt-and-gathering,
one's for sorrow, two's a sign of joy.

Points of light pinprick the velvet sky
stitching back and forth, a tapestry:
One's for sorrow, two's a sign of joy
to clothe the entire earth in majesty.

Stitching back and forth, a tapestry
the wind sighs once, a solitary leaf drops
to clothe the entire earth in majesty
as clouds cover sleeping suburban rooftops.

2024

I Stand with the Trees

I stand with the trees:
Tall trees in shadowed valleys,
sapling and mighty oak,
whose particoloured canopies
fall like an autumn cloak.

I stand with the stones:
Carved sandstone and pink granite
encircling the earth
beneath whose shelter, in complete
rest, bones await rebirth.

I stand with the still:
Those lost in contemplation
who have left behind the world.
I stand for the sure, slow progress
of a bracken fern, unfurled.

2024

Beachcombing

Beachcombing
Thursday morning
the tide pools in between
the land and sea.
Sweet seaweed scents
enhance my sense
of wonder, renewed by earth's wild beauty.

Rock-hopping
at the landing-
site of cormorants
drying their outstretched wings
where barnacles
and mussel shells
line crevices with other treasured things.

I'm dancing
Sunday morning
in a watercolour
painted by the sand,
ribbed, like the sky
whose clouds roll by
to cobalt blue the ochre of the land.

I'm dreaming
about painting

the ocean, with its fervour,
and its froth.
But for an artist's eye and hand
I'd render both the sky and land:
The glory and the splendour of the earth.

2024

Shunyata

I am the wind, rippling the reed-beds,
causing cotton-grass to sigh;
I am a tall and stately mountain
ten miles high.

I am a cloud of cotton billow
when the spring is on the wane;
I am a summer morning meadow
washed with rain.

I am the North Sea tide, receding,
bleeding seashells on the shore
constantly in flux, but never
needing more.

2024

Along the Winding Trail

Along the winding trail
there's ice and mud to blemish boots,
whispers of fairytale,
river-wrecks and gnarled tree roots,
heron stands sentinel.

Along the winding trail, I'm very happy
even when the trail is marred
by heels, and waste—footprints of heavy industry
heaven's gates are barred.

Beyond the winding trail
only an expanse of sky
and sun
and sleeping stars.

2025

Mulholland Drive is Burning

Mulholland Drive is burning,
a curtain of smoke descends upon L.A.
"We're wild at heart, and weird on top,"
keep dancing anyway.

The Black Lodge and the White Lodge,
the Wicked and the Good,
the twisted and the trusted
are the most misunderstood:

The portal gates are open
an owl hoots overhead,
another boulevard, a star in heaven:
David Lynch is dead.

2025

The Engraver's Art

I ride out to sea, to see
the broad sweep of the Bay,
the curves carved into every cove,
the seabirds all at play,

to hear the songs sung by the tide:
The heave, and roar, and moan
which, pounding on the cliff's broadside
makes sand from solid stone,

the wail and whisper of the sedge
swept by the east wind's sigh,
the burnished copper of the hedge
etched on the lead-lined sky.

All this, and more, I see each day
that I ride out to sea:
Such is The Engraver's Art recalled
in lines of poetry.

2025

Emily

Over the mutinous moors the wind blows
harshly,
over the sighing slope falls ragged rain,
ragged, like your breathing,
seething, seeming rashly
railed against the fates
aligned in pain.

In through the churchyard gate come mourners,
solemn,
two sisters and a brother sleep below
the marble slab, and pillar-vaulted column
those lives which passed too fast,
as grief, too slow.

To those left standing by the wooden casket
narrow like your cast, not like your mind
which seemed to know no fetters, and no limit:
Boundless as the screaming eastern wind.

What magic words you left us
sleeping sister!
What barren, blasted heath,
what wilderness!
What searing passions swell beneath and blister
through your maiden cloak of girlishness?

What epitaph of mine could ever praise you
in terms befitting all the words you wrought?
I have not art to resurrect or raise you
above the earth and your small sleeping plot

so I'll end with a prayer of benediction
and tell you all the world knows your words' worth
kindled within the foundry fires of passion
now sleeping soundly in the quiet earth.

2025

Last Ride before Easter

The sea is a flat, grey sheet:
Dull and flat as my low mood,
ruffled on the surface
while beyond
a kestrel, the colour of weathered sandstone
points her head into the wind
continuing, and hovers.

Then the next day, spring returns,
and with it, all the joy into my heart
unhurried yet still hopeful
while a daffodil, in our back yard
unfolds its yellows to the glaring sun
uncovered.

And all the colours seem in sharper focus,
as if this were the last day of my life:
I love the daylight and its sounds
and smoke-smell on the air,
and all the scents which hover there,
the way the church spire chimes
with sun and shadow

An etched image of the divine,
topped by a weathervane—
a cross carved in the Saviour's name

before Palm Sunday.

April 2025

Petrarchan Sonnet

There's blossom on the bough again, my love
and every tree puts forth new shoots of green,
as often I have seen
along the path within the wooded grove

hidden beside the stream: A treasure trove
of orange, gold, all colours in between
as in a dream
the flowers sway below the sky above.

I watch the silent turning of the year
and wonder at the round of nature's dance
at spring's entrance

while winds and waters which have brought me here
combine to stir
quiet passion into wild romance.

2025

Of Molehills…

Of molehills and daffodils,
primroses and bluebells,
coming home in springtime to your arms.

Of daisy chains and weathervanes,
moaning March winds, April rains,
Palm Sunday singing from the Book of Psalms.

Of tide wracks and beach rocks,
ice cream, town hall clocks
and hidden trails along the midden heights.

Of bluestones and new moons,
seaweeds and sand dunes,
from fragrant days to heaven-scented nights.

From sea walls, the birdcalls
of starlings and seagulls
reach seals resting on rocks in peace

while lovers of flowers
may while away hours
welcome to the hum of the bees.

2025

Wholly Holy Island

Wholly Holy Island
I belong
to your turf walls and buttered earth, I cling:
Cleave to your crumbling priory,
behind your ancient library,
within your empty, cloistered halls
I sing.

Wholly Holy Island
I've been gone
where wild winds blow, enough to know I've come
back your mystic liminals,
your sea-frets and subliminals,
Wholly Holy Island
I am home.

Wholly Holy Island
this I know,
from standing on your shore,
where wild winds blow
over your dunes and castle-hill,
over the land, the sea, the thrill:
Wholly Holy Island
this is so.

2025

Streets of Dreaming

Streets of dreaming,
pavement slabs and cobbled roads,
redbrick houses, terraced
beds of slate-grey clouds.

Streaks of lightning
split the sky on summer nights
spilling over onto guttered
rooftops, silver slates.

Golden mornings
bathe the river, venerate the hills
rise above the building sites,
factories, farms, and silent mills.

Summer sleeping
shuttered out, the late night sun
comes on waking
lingers on all through the dawn.

Bold, believing
that a certain time or place
can be captured
or might ever leave a trace

in the evening
with the rising harvest moon
of our leaving
whispered memories of June.

2025

A Bracken Fern

For me, a bracken fern,
no laurel crown:
No laureate,
no punditry,
no plaudits.

Only a line of hills,
a wild rose bush,
a bramble thorn,
a surging sea
encircling stone:
Pink granite.

A heath,
a hillside
and a grove of gorse
flown over by
a gaggle of wild geese,
a bouldered barrow
bordered by blue stones
encircling the sleeper's silent bones.

A kestrel, who hovers spirit-like, above
the clifftops and the bracken-covered grove
while a song, clear as the early morning light
awakens sleeping strains of deep delight

in a graveyard graced with bluebells whose heads, bowed
drop pollen tears upon the fertile ground
as bracken ferns unfurl their bannered green
to clothe the hillside and these bones of mine.

2025

Child of the Wild High Places

Child of the wild high places
where rocks, wind-carved like faces
overlook a never-ending scene
I stand, serene.

Child of the nooks and crannies
hidden corners, passageways and alleys
lead to secret palaces
timeless and traceless.

Child of expansive waters,
lakeland paradises, sea-swept daughter's
dancing on the sand,
just so, I stand.

Child of the changing seasons
collecting poetry, and rhyming reasons
just to be still a while,
only to smile.

2025

Through Rising Tides

*"The cistern contains, the fountain overflows"—Blake,
Proverbs of Hell*

Through rising tides
and falling stars,
through picture-books
and moonbeams:
A voice which travels from afar
and reaches me in dreams.

The Muse of all the earth and sky,
the Ark of ancient wisdom,
captured in clouds which drift on by
to sleep beneath my bosom.

Bluest of blues
in all the world
I had not yet imagined
any such hues, so bright, so bold
indelibly ink-stained.

Dream of a dream
of ancient lands,
hidden deserts and mountains,
through chambered rock
and secret sands

the hourglass contains.

The glass contains,
then overflows:
I cannot hope to hold it
enough to watch its troughs, its plows
enough that I have told it.

2025

Long Live "No-neck"

Long live "No-neck"
the jombling Geordie
pounding the pavements of Monkseaton drive,
hound held and lead-led
and smiling because he's alive.

Long live the seagulls
harassing the people
who dare to eat chips on the seafront each day of July.
Long live the seals on the rocks
and the clouds sailing by.

Here's to the ice-cream vans,
kiosks and coffee-stands
and all the children who scrabble for crabs on the rocks.
Here's to time-telling by tides
not the ticking of clocks.

Here's to St Mary's
adorning the headland
chalked out against
storm-gathered skies:
Here's to the lovers who hold hands
beneath her, change eyes.

2025

If I Could Paint the Colours of your Eyes

If I could paint the colours of your eyes,
I fantasise, I'd swim that depth of blue
and what I wouldn't do
to bring the sparkle back when it has fled,
to lift your heart when it's dispirited.

If I could paint the glory of a dream,
how would it seem, if painted perfectly?
And how would you find me:
A creature of your own imagining,
or something else, unknown and challenging?

If I could paint the colours of sunset,
I'd paint a realm of infinite delight
engraved in evening light
to reach you with a burst of evensong
which lingers as it echoes, all night long.

2025

Unlearned

With all the things that I have learned
unlearned
and all the things I might have said
unsaid,
high in a mountain cave, silent
beyond the watershed
skirting the border of the living world,

breathing the stillness of a mirrored pool,
through mists of sunrise valleys hid below
the stones begin to spin, and reel, and spool
revealing what was hidden long ago:

It lies forgotten in your centred heart,
it was forgotten when you learned to speak it,
it hides whenever you reach for it with art,
it disappears from everywhere you seek it.

So do not look for it, in cave or cove,
forget false witness of remembering.
Forget your quest, for, in this world of love
all things return in time to their beginning.

2025

Banded

Banded together
through eons of weather
through hell or high water
those sons of a daughter
have seen all
and been all
through sun and through rainfall
and still shall
in time tell
all time to a standstill
yet moving
and spinning
from end to beginning
and over and over
for ever
and ever.

2025

Devoke

Mirror on the world above,
slate grey
stone, carved
with time and love,
this portal to a higher realm
soothes sleepers, whose ancestral home
is hidden, high above the hordes
and grazed by the unknowing herds
who gambol by the silent stones
unwittingly, they guard the bones
still sleeping in this fertile earth:
Foetal, an other-worldly birth.

And this place is evocative
of those who think to love and live
beneath a sky of coloured clouds
highlighted by such shifting shrouds,
yet never shackled by the fears
of time, and other worldly cares:
They dream of otherworldly realms
while stone-wall circles guard their dreams.

2025

The Quickening

Skiddaw is a sundial,
the desolate beauty of the Solway plain
lit with a half-smile,
harvest of clouds forecasting rain.

The desolate beauty of the Solway plain
butterflies dance the breeze,
harvest of clouds forecasting rain,
cars hum like bumblebees.

Butterflies dance the breeze,
tabletop mountain stands,
cars hum like bumblebees
over these wild marshlands.

Tabletop mountain stands,
I'm out there somewhere too
over these wild marshlands
gathering honey dew.

I'm out there somewhere too,
Skiddaw is a sundial
gathering honey dew,
lit with a half-smile.

2025

Softly, over Skiddaw

Softly, over Skiddaw
the evening sun descends
through the pasture, down the meadow,
after summer ends:
Where the hillside meets the reedbed
and the river bends.

Gently, over Jedburgh
gorgeous palaces of clouds
tumble wildly, woven blindly
into evening shrouds
by a hidden, cloistered spinster
far from careless crowds.

Evenings, over Eden,
on the cusp of spring
past the Pennines, to the Solway
hosts of sparrows sing
songs of rebirth, songs of joy
beyond imagining.

Softly, over Skiddaw
the evening sun descends
through the pasture, down the meadow,
as the river bends:
Where the hillside meets the reedbed

and the light transcends.

2025

Publication Credits

'Poem on Your Birthday' and 'My Father's Garden' first published in *40 Poems at 40* (EIF, 2022).

'Sorry Mate' first published in *But You Don't Look Sick* (Indie Blu(e), 2021).

'Slow Sleepwalk into Armageddon' and 'Jellyfish Jam' first published in *The Anthropocene Hymnal* (EIF, 2021).

'Points North' first published by Spillwords Press, August 2020.

'Serpentine' first published in Visual Verse, Volume 8, May 2021.

'Persephone' first published in Free Verse Revolution, Issue IV, December 2021.

'Star of Wonder' first published by Spillwords Press, December 2021.

'A Thimble of Poetry' and 'Dawn Resonance,' first published in *Archery in the UK* (EIF, 2023).

'If You Kill the Bird,' 'Winter's Margin,' and 'Watershed' first published in *To Catch a Poem* (EIF, 2023).

'Oddendale' first published in *New Lyricist* magazine, Issue 1, Winter 2024.

Also Available from EIF

To Catch A Poem
by Ingrid Wilson
ISBN: 9781739404475

From Bannerdale to Bewcastle, Cullercoats to Caldbeck, poet Ingrid Wilson criss-crosses the Northern countryside, searching for lines of poetry hidden in high places and wooded hollows. Nature is her place of worship, and poetry her song of praise.

Archery in the UK
by Nick Reeves and Ingrid Wilson
ISBN: 9781739757786

Inspired by the *Lyrical Ballads* of Wordsworth and Coleridge, two authors set out to pen a contemporary homage to this timeless collection. As the collaboration progresses, however, the poetry and the narrative it carries takes on a life of its own. Thus, the authors come to tell a love story through this collection of ballads, sonnets and other forms.

Three-Penny Memories, A Poetic Memoir
by Barbara Harris Leonhard
ISBN: 9781739757762

"Do you love your mother?" This provocative question provides the catalyst for this stunning poetic memoir from Pushcart Nominee Barbara Harris Leonhard, who considers where her loyalties lie following her mother's diagnosis with Alzheimer's.

All Grown Up Now
by Kim M. Russell
ISBN: 9781739404437

This collection shows what it was like to grow up in a family in the decades after the war, how it shapes the individual, what they learn and keep in their heart, and the rituals and routines that are handed down the generations.

40 Poems At 40
by Ingrid Wilson
ISBN: 9781739757700

40 Poems is the debut poetry collection from Ingrid Wilson. It is poetry of place and space, and here lie the clues and the beauty to Wilson's poetry. Her work is charted, landscaped, travelled, explorative and laden with adventure.

www.ingramcontent.com/pod-product-compliance
Lightning Source LLC
Chambersburg PA
CBHW071249070526
44583CB00017B/2391